I LIKE THE

DEPRESSION

Learning how to make your own chicken soup in troubled times

David Okerlund

with

Misti Okerlund

Library of Congress Control Number: 2009908259
ISBN: Hardcover   978-1-4415-6375-0
               Softcover   978-1-4415-6374-3

This book was printed in the United States of America.

To order additional copies of this book, contact:
Xlibris Corporation
1-888-795-4274
www.Xlibris.com
Orders@Xlibris.com
63136

I LIKE THE DEPRESSION

CONTENTS

Dedication

This book is dedicated to Sally Wall's father—a man I wish
I could have met. Although he died nearly forty-five years ago,
his legacy still shines brightly today.

An Initial Thought

I always like to remind my readers of something said long ago in England where a common man rose to greatness in the British Parliament. His name was Sir Fowell Buxton or cherishingly noted by friends and foes alike as "Elephant Buxton" for both his stature and his renowned resolution and perseverance.

One of the pursuits that he focused his great energy upon was his reading. He worked through the day and gave up his evenings to the readings and subsequent digestion of English law and the great authors. In particular, his maxims for reading impacted the format of this book. They were simple but profoundly productive.

"Never to begin a book without finishing it."
"Never to consider a book finished until it is mastered."
"Study everything with the whole mind."

Special Note to the Reader:

It's not often that a writer gets the opportunity I received while working on this book. In the process of trying to make this work as relevant and rewarding as possible, serendipity came into play when my daughter-in-law volunteered to help me edit the book. Although she is a very successful practicing attorney, she is a great editor as well.

However, within weeks she became even more vital to the effort. Misti soon moved from editing to contributing. Her thoughts helped to keep this project on track and relevant to more than just my generation.

INTRODUCTION

When you squeeze an orange, you get orange juice. You never get apple juice or tomato juice. When anything (or anyone) is under pressure, their true essence comes out. When times are good, people can 'invent' their outward appearance. When times are tough, you get to see what's really inside.

—Unknown

Let me preface what you are about to read by telling you that I, like many people my age, grew up hearing many horror stories about the Great Depression. My grandfather would relentlessly tell us, "You better hope and pray you never have to see another depression. It wasn't just the bottom of the barrel—it was beneath the bottom of the barrel. It was the closest thing to hell on earth you will ever see." I grew up fearing a depression almost as much as death itself.

Then, a number of years ago, I came across a simple piece of literature that changed my entire attitude about life and the tough times we all occasionally have to face. It wasn't found in a great book of poetry or a literary masterpiece. It was found in 1965 when Sally Wall's father passed away somewhere in the Midwest. She found it tucked away in his wallet. The note was scribbled on a little piece of paper. The title was *I Like the Depression* and was dated 1932—the very heart of the depression era. Here is the version I discovered:

> I like the depression. No more prosperity for me. I have had more fun since the depression started than I ever had in my entire life. You see, I had forgotten how to live, and what it meant to have real friends, and what it was like to eat common, everyday food. Fact is, I was getting a little too high-hat.
>
> I like the depression. It's great to drop into a store and feel that you can spend an hour or two visiting and not feel that you are wasting valuable time.
>
> I like the depression. I am getting acquainted with my neighbors and following the biblical admonition to love them. Some of them had been living next door to me for years, and I didn't see them. Now we even get together and butcher a few hogs.
>
> I like the depression. I haven't been out to a party in eighteen months. My wife has dropped all her clubs, and I believe we are falling in love all over again. I'm pretty well satisfied with my wife, and I think I will keep her. (You can tell that was written in 1932.)
>
> I am feeling better since the depression started. I get more exercise because I now walk to town. However, a lot of folks who used to drive Cadillacs are walking with me.
>
> I like the depression. I am getting real, honest-to-goodness food now. Three years ago we had filet of sole, crab louie, and Swiss steak with flour gravy. We had guinea hens and things called "gourmet" and "oriental." Now, we eat sow bellies with the buttons still on them!
>
> I like the depression. Three years ago I never had time to go to church. I played checkers or baseball all day

Sunday. Besides, there wasn't a preacher that could tell me anything. Now, I'm going to church regularly and never miss a Sunday. If this Depression keeps on, I will be going to prayer meetings before too long.

Oh, yes! I like the depression!

Think about that for a few moments. Here was a man, standing in one of the greatest pits of darkness in the history of America, and he chose to see the light. He was able to find the best of times in the very center of the worst. Sally Wall's father had a mind-set that allowed him to make the most of what he had to work with. In essence, he made his own chicken soup, and that's what this book is all about.

PREFACE

Our lives are filled with moments when we have to make choices. Some of them are small and insignificant, and some of them profoundly affect our lives. The key component is the fact that we are individually responsible for making those choices. Reading this book is one of the choices you have just made, and if you read it with an open mind, I believe it will be a great decision. I believe that all major paradigm shifts that take place in our lives begin with the first step of making a choice. The following poem perhaps best illustrates that point.

Choices

In between . . .
That moment of birth,
And the day
When the hands of time
Will cease to move again

In between . . .
That which we are given,
Over which we have no control.
And that which we will contribute,
But must leave behind.

In between . . .
The initial light and the final darkness.
The first cry and the last farewell,
The moments of glory and bitter sorrow,
The victories and the defeats,

The highs and the lows,
The laughter and the tears,
The seconds and the years,

In between . . .
This magnificent sea of experiences,
There is but one critical control;
One mighty linchpin of destiny
That not even God can take away from you!

For in between, my friend . . .
You have choices.

When I really began to study those words written long ago by Mr. Wall, I discovered six poignant choices that I believe he made which helped him rise above the tragedy of those depression years. Although they were great choices then, they still are today regardless of our individual circumstances in life. In essence, his words were and are a great road map for living a great life. I hope you enjoy them. At the end of each chapter, you will also find several recipes for making your own batch of chicken soup on the subjects covered.

(Picture from the Franklin D. Roosevelt Library, courtesy of the National Archives and Records Administration.)

Choice #1

TRIM YOUR PRIDE

Choice #1

TRIM YOUR PRIDE

Pride attaches undue importance to the superiority of one's status in the eyes of others; And shame is fear of humiliation at one's inferior status in the estimation of others. When one sets his heart on being highly esteemed, and achieves such rating, then he is automatically involved in fear of losing his status.

—Lao Tzu

If there are two human characteristics that seem to show up together more than any other, they are pride and greed. One almost always pursues the other in the back alleys of our hearts and minds. I am not talking about the kind of pride one might have for being a proud father or a proud American. There's nothing wrong with being proud about doing a good job, whether it's obtaining a special degree or a task like landscaping your yard. That kind of pride is wholesome and deserves our self-appreciation.

The kind of pride I am referring to is the pride that puts us above others. It's the kind that whispers, "I'll bet they are looking at me now." You see, it's not the person who strives to dress well who bothers me. It's the person who strives to dress well because he or she wants everyone to notice how good they look. That kind of pride is like a cancer—when it begins to grow, it is forever hungry for more and will spread into every realm of our attitude.

For many years America has been cruising on the Ship of Plenty in the Sea of Prosperity. The sky was the only limit. We bought bigger homes and went from one-stall garages to three and even four. Overnight, we transitioned from a cheap six-pack of beer to Johnny Walker Black scotch and expensive microbrews. Instead of going to the city for a weekend, we suddenly found ourselves jumping on a plane for a quick weekend in Vegas. I met a young woman who told me that she and her husband spent $20,000 remodeling their kitchen, and in the last six months since it was finished, they had yet to cook an evening dinner at home! The list could go on and on.

However, in 2008, an economic tsunami swept across America and changed everything. And when I am counseling individuals who are having a tough time adapting to less, I inevitably find that their greatest problem in making those necessary changes is their battle with their sense of pride. C.S. Lewis once said, "Pride gets no pleasure out of having something, only out of having more of it than the next man." Unfortunately, pride puts up a pretty strong battle. It's hard to say "I'll pass" when your friends want to go out for cocktails and dinner at a restaurant you know you can't afford. For some it's easier to cave in and dump another $100 onto their already overextended credit card. It's not easy to tell your kids you can't afford to send them on an Easter break to Cancun. It's never easy unless you learn to trim your pride. But it can be done.

My suggestions are really quite simple. The best way to defeat pride is to disarm it before a confrontation begins. Take a stand today, and take the stand at home first and next with your friends. Just tell those you care about that you are cutting back and are going to be more prudent on how you spend your money. It's really no different than telling them you've been eating too much lately and are going on a diet. In reality, most of them are probably in the same boat and will welcome your stand. I'm not saying it's wrong to treat yourself to a cup of gourmet coffee every now and then. Just be a little more prudent in how you spend your discretionary money on a daily basis.

Try going to a Goodwill Store every other week, and stay there until you find something you can wear. Then, go to work the next day, and show your friends the incredible bargain you found. I had a friend who did that, and three other people at his work site asked him to give them a call the next time he went there so they could join him. The next time you are tempted to buy another shirt or blouse or jacket at your favorite high-end department store, count the shirts that are already hanging in your closet and ask yourself if you truly need another.

Buy a cookbook of your favorite cuisine, pick out three simple recipes you think you might like, and stay home three nights each week eating your own culinary delights. If you haven't done any cooking before, be prepared for a few disasters along the way, but when they happen, don't rush out to a restaurant. Instead, find satisfaction with a bowl of cereal or a fried egg sandwich. And if you keep at it, someday your spouse or significant other might turn to you and say what my wife said to me a number of years ago: "Honey, you are truly a gourmet cook!" Why pay twenty-eight dollars for a fillet at a restaurant when you can grill the same steak for twelve dollars on your home grill?

What's more, you can make it fun. Jump on your computer, and design your own reward card for cooking at home. At the bottom of the card, print the numbers one to five. Now each time you create your own culinary delight for dinner, punch out one of the numbers. When you have punched out all five numbers, reward yourself with an evening out. And remember—have your predinner cocktail at home so you don't have to pay premium prices when you get to your chosen restaurant.

Doing things like this will not banish your pride away forever, but they will help keep it from manipulating you. As the French author, Francis de La Rochefoucauld, once said, "A shrewd man has to arrange his interests in order of importance and deal with them one by one; but often our greed upsets this order and makes us run after so many things at once that through over-anxiety to obtain the trivial, we miss the most important."

Let me give you an example from my own life. Luckily, I have been married to one of the greatest women on the face of the planet. She is special in a hundred different ways, but one of the most unique aspects about Twila is her ability to live without the ogre of pride. She has never been obsessed with wearing jewelry. Twila buys about 75 percent of her clothes at the Opportunity Village Store in our town, which is the equivalent of a Goodwill Store. She maintains a nice home, but many of the furnishings are secondhand pieces as well. And yet when you see her, she looks like an angel—simple and yet glowing. Her self-esteem isn't centered on how she looks. It's centered on how she feels inside.

Twila is an RN at our regional hospital where she specializes in diabetes education. When she heads out the drive each morning, she is driving a 1998 Chevy Blazer, which I refer to as the "rust bucket." We bought it used and unfortunately did not know that the previous owner had done a quick "bondo and paint" job to conceal the rust, which completely surrounded the lower level of the vehicle. Needless to say, six months later the rust returned and spread like crabgrass on an untended lawn.

I want to dump the vehicle and get her something better. But not Twila. She insists the car runs smoothly and is dependable. It has four-wheel drive to see her safely through the Iowa snowstorms and is gas efficient. She intends to drive it as long as it serves her well. That was five years ago, and she still loves the deformed, unsightly beast today. However, every now and then when I have to drive her car downtown to join my friends at the corner coffee shop, I find myself looking for a parking place around the corner and down the block. Why? You guessed it: pride. I realize this might sound a little trivial, but it isn't to me. For me, it's a reminder that my battle with pride is still going on.

To me, pride is like the tiny flakes of dust that are relentless in their pursuit to find a place in our house. I'm never sure where they come from, and at first I don't even notice them. But they are there, and they have a propensity to cover every piece of furniture and fixture in the place. Finally, I have to get out the Pledge and go to work on them. Pride also quietly creeps into our lives and every now and then needs a little housekeeping. One of the ways I do that is to pull out one of my favorite poems.

THE MAN IN THE GLASS

When you get what you want in your struggle for self
And the world makes you king for a day,
Then go up to the mirror and look at yourself
And see what that guy has to say.

For it isn't your father or mother or wife whom
Upon you their judgment will pass.
But the fellow whose verdict counts most in your life
Is the one staring back in the glass.

You may be like Jack Horner and chisel a plum
And think you're a wonderful guy.
But the guy in the glass says you are only a bum
If you can't look him straight in the eye.

He's the fellow to please, never mind all the rest,
For he's with you clear up to the end.
And so then you've passed your most difficult test
If the man in the glass is your friend.

You can fool the world down the pathways of years
And get pats on the back as you pass.
But your final reward will be heartaches and tears
If you've cheated that man in the glass

Anonymous

Maybe one of the most positive things about these troubled times is the fact that many, if not most of us, are forced to eat a piece or two of humble pie. Fortunately, once you've done it, it is not all that hard. Don't worry—it won't give you a case of mental indigestion. As another friend of mine says, "Eating humble pie is like getting ready for a colonoscopy. It's tough to swallow, but it certainly does clean out your system."

No one ever choked to death swallowing their pride.

—Unknown

A few recipes for trimming one's pride

• Go to an office supply store and buy a small packet of colored stick-on circles. They are about the size of a quarter. Take one out and place it in the front corner of your credit or debit card. Then, each time you are about to purchase something, look at the colored circle and ask yourself this question: "Am I buying this item because I need it, or am I buying it because it will make me look good?" If the answer is the latter, have the humility to return the item to the shelf where you found it.

• This one was not easy for a lot of my male friends to accept, let alone try, but I guarantee it is a great recipe for adding a little humility to your life if you are struggling with pride. Spend two weeks going through your daily newspaper and cut out every coupon you see for items you typically buy. At the end of the second week, volunteer to do the grocery shopping, and when you get to the checkout counter, use as many of the coupons you can. You would be surprised how many individuals have trouble doing this.

• The next time you are invited over to someone's house for dinner and you decide to bring along a bottle of wine, resist the pride of paying $25 for a bottle of Coppola's Diamond Series and buy something like a $7 bottle of Yellow Tail Shiraz. It they are like most people, they too have their own favorite, less-expensive wines they enjoy and shouldn't take offense.

• Read the following verse and then write down several sentences of what you think it is trying to tell you about your life.

BE THE BEST OF WHATEVER YOU ARE

If you can't be a pine on the top of the hill
Be a scrub in the valley but be
The best little scrub by the side of the hill
Be a bush if you can't be a tree

If you can't be a bush, be a bit of grass
And some highway happier make
If you can't be a muskie, then just be a bass
But be the liveliest bass in the lake
We can't all be captains, we've got to be crew
There is something for all of us
There is big work to do and there's lesser to do
And the task we must do is near

If you can't be a highway, then just be the trail
If you can't be the sun, be a star
For it isn't by size that you win or you fail,
But rather being the best of whatever you are.

Douglas Mallock

(Picture from the Franklin D. Roosevelt Library, courtesy of the
National Archives and Records Administration.)

Choice #2

SIMPLIFY YOUR LIFE

Choice #2

SIMPLIFY YOUR LIFE

A little simplification would be the first step toward rational living, I think.

—Eleanor Roosevelt

I have learned by some experience, by many examples, and by the writings of countless others before me, also occupied in the search, that certain environments, certain modes of life, certain rules of conduct are more conducive to inner and outer harmony than others. There are, in fact, certain roads that one may follow. Simplification of life is one of them.

—Anne Morrow Lindbergh

Let me be perfectly blunt: clutter is to one's peace of mind as plaque is to one's blood stream. Most of us are affected by it because most of us were drawn into it by the incredible period of prosperity we experienced in the past. If we wanted something, we got it, and when we got it, we had to make room for it. And with the ongoing, unrelenting advancements that paved this great interstate of prosperity, it wasn't long before someone came up with a newer or better version of what we already had. So what did we do? We got it and buried the earlier version in a desk drawer or closet.

In another book I recently wrote, *Managing the Margins of Greatness*, I referred to this malady as the "Got-to-Get Syndrome." The obsession ranges from everything like the progression of bulky mobile phones to Razor cell phones, from VHS machines to DVDs, from simple computers to BlackBerrys, from small TVs to sixty-inch plasma-screen digital giants with surround sound and all the other accessories.

Just take a mental tour through your home. How many televisions can you find? How many CDs do you own? How many coats and jackets are hanging in the closet or on the coat rack? How many kitchen appliances do you own which haven't been used in the last month? How many pieces of body building equipment are gathering dust?

For me, this is not an easy chapter to write because with every sentence typed, I'm faced with another conviction. As I am sitting in front of the computer right now, there is a two-stall garage outside my front door, which hasn't seen a car parked in it for the last three years. Today, it is more of a warehouse than a garage. It's stuffed with antique furniture that will never be refinished or used. There are about fifty different power tools, most of which I couldn't find. However, that's no problem because over 50 percent of those same tools I will probably never use. I can't move stuff up into the rafters because the rafters are currently strained to their limits with more stuff my children left behind for us to keep until they found room for them. That was about fifteen years ago.

Several months ago, if you had taken a brief tour of our home, you would have discovered more of the same. I could have opened closet doors where you would have found boxes of more stuff, dozens of pictures we no longer hang on the walls, and clothes which haven't been worn in the last five years. In my office you could have found at least five old tape recorders, three computers, two printers, over one hundred books collecting dust, two chairs on which only the dogs sleep, an AB Lounger 2 that now serves as a clothes rack, two video cameras, three tripods, over one hundred video tapes no one will ever watch, a towering antique file cabinet which hasn't been opened in the last two years, and a Pro Form Crosswalk treadmill that I am proud to admit is being used. Unfortunately, this was only a partial list. Finally, I decided to take action. It was a painful process at first, but as time and progress took place, it became easier. I kept reflecting on Henry David Thoreau's words, "Our life is frittered away by detail . . . Simplify, simplify, simplify! . . . Simplicity of life and elevation of purpose." And you know something? He was right.

The point I'm trying to make is that there's nothing wrong with any of these items on an individual basis. I'm not against computers or books, but as the piles increase they become a form of mental and spiritual plaque. It's like barnacles growing on a boat. The boat can still navigate through the water, but the ride eventually becomes less smooth because the boat loses its balance. It's much like a cluttered desk. There are some of us who take pride in the clutter. It says we are busy, and we swear we know where everything is in the pile. Then one day it reaches a point where we can't kid ourselves anymore. It's a jungle, and we hate walking into that jungle every morning because we know we are going to get lost.

A great solution to the physical clutter is reflected in the rule we now live by. If it hasn't been used in the last two years, get rid of it. Have a garage sale. Take it to Goodwill and get a nice donation receipt. If it's a duplicate of something newer and you don't have a justified reason for keeping it as a backup, get rid of it. If you have not worn it in the last three years, regardless of what you originally paid for it, give it to a friend or sell it on eBay. I have a friend whose wife just can't pass up a great shirt sale at JCPenney. So, when the 50 percent off shows up and she has a coupon for an additional 15 percent off, she buys several shirts for him. He told me one day he decided to count the shirts in his closet and those still unwrapped on the shelves. He counted seventy-eight different dress shirts, and yet there are only five or six he consistently wears.

However, when I am talking about simplifying your life, I'm not just talking about material stuff. There's the emotional, psychological, and spiritual side as well. One of the most cherished memories I have about my grandparents is a ritual that was part of their everyday life. After supper each night, Grandpa would leave the supper table and go into the living room. He sat down in an old rocking chair with one of those black velvet pillows on the seat. Next to the rocking chair stood a floor magazine rack, cradling six old Arizona Highway Magazines. Over the years they never changed, but that didn't seem to bother Grandpa. He would simply sit down, peruse the selection, and make his pick. Then he would browse through the magazine until a picture captured his attention. It was like a window of serenity had been opened up for him. And so, for the next forty-five minutes, Grandpa would drift off into a journey that seemed to bring a special peace of mind to his countenance. The muscles in his neck would relax. The tension in his body from a day of arduous labor would dissipate. Gradually, the man of stone would become a gentle teddy bear before our silent, reverent eyes. I call it, "Obtaining the Grace of Receptivity."

For the longest time I marveled at, but didn't understand, what he was doing. For a ten-year-old boy, it was a ritual, shrouded in mystery, never explained by Grandma, but ardently respected and not intruded upon by anyone. When it was over, we could pile onto Grandpa and play, but never before he had completed his sojourn.

Now I realize what Grandpa was doing each and every night. He was emptying the bucket. He was mentally and spiritually processing the negative barnacles he had accumulated during that day's labor. Simple? Yes. Trite? Maybe. But as simple and trite as it might sound, it had a profound effect on his internal equilibrium.

Perhaps the greatest parallel to what I am trying to say is best reflected in our observance to the "Day of Rest" we once cherished in our lives and families. It was what my great grandfather referred to as "the Holy Sabbath." My grandfather called it "the Sabbath." My father called it "Sunday." But today we simply refer to it as "the weekend." Understand this: as strongly as I feel about the importance of faith, I am not addressing this from a religious perspective. Rather, I would like you to consider the following observation from strictly a self-management point of view.

There will soon come a time, if it has not already arrived, when very few people will understand the term "Blue Laws." That term represented a law, observed by most states in America starting in the colonial days and finally fading from enforcement during the mid-1900s, by which almost every business in the country was forced to shut down for a day. That day was Sunday. Unless it concerned the need for emergency medicine, virtually every place of business was shut down. The clothing stores were closed on Sunday. The grocery stores were closed on Sunday. On Sundays, most main streets looked like ghost towns. Although the Blue Laws had a religious genesis, the intent was to give everyone a day of rest. It wasn't another day for commerce, but rather, a day for families. The result was the fact that an awful lot of garbage was processed on Sundays. Unfortunately, after World War II, we built the Turnpike of Success in America but forgot to build any rest stops and very few exits. So most of us are racing down the turnpike, bumper to bumper, not realizing the void we are creating internally.

Daniel Webster said, "The longer I live the more highly I estimate the Christian Sabbath, and the more grateful do I feel to those who impress its importance on the community."

Tryon Edwards said, "To say nothing of the divine law, on mere worldly grounds it is plain that nothing is more conducive to the health, intelligence, comfort, and independence than our Christian American Sabbath."

Henry Ward Beecher said, "A world without a Sabbath would be like a man without a smile, like a summer without flowers, and like a homestead without a garden. It is the joyous day of the whole week." It was the day of the big family dinner get-together after going to church. It was an afternoon to go for a ride with the family in the country. It was a day of leisurely conversations, perhaps a few rounds of croquet in the back yard, and the infamous Sunday-afternoon nap Mom and Dad took together, sometimes on the couch and sometimes, strangely, behind a closed bedroom door no child ever dreamed of disturbing. For almost all Americans, Sunday was once a great and gloriously observed rest stop on the Turnpike of Success. We shut down our engines, refilled our spiritual and emotional gas tanks, and cleaned off the dirt that had begun to blur our windshields to the world.

Wow! What a difference forty years can have. And ironically, we call this progress. No wonder we have become a nation of gladiators. No wonder we have so many people stepping into emotional sinkholes. The Grace of Receptivity is a cornerstone to mental and spiritual health. It is that internal reservoir—the underground river that feeds our enrichment and wellness. However, for many Americans, that river has become nothing less than a void, no longer able to hold up what is above. And voids are the prerequisites to sinkholes.

Let me just ask you a few questions that will quickly tell you how full your internal reservoir is.

• Do you set aside at least thirty minutes each day for just yourself . . . to embrace the restorative bliss of silence?
• When was the last time you sat and listened to a pensive, spirit-lifting album?
• When was the last time you spent an hour or so by yourself, reading and contemplating the words in your "Good Book", whatever that "Good Book" might be?

These are all times set aside just for you . . . To empty the bucket . . . To restore, renew, and replenish. Your answer might well define how much harmony there is within your life.

As a speaker friend of mine, the late Og Mandino, once said, "Never again clutter your days or nights with so many menial and unimportant things that you have no time to accept a real challenge when it comes along. This applies to play as well as work. A day merely survived is no cause for celebration. You are not here to fritter away your precious hours when you have the ability to accomplish so much by making a slight change in your routine. No more busy work. No more hiding from success. Leave time, leave space, to grow. Now. Now! Not tomorrow!"

How do we go about finding and embracing simplification? I sincerely believe that the first step is to accept ourselves for what we are, nothing more and nothing less. We can't even begin to think about making great recipes for chicken soup for ourselves or others if we do not accept ourselves as unique and gifted individuals with the potential of arising from wherever we currently reside to a higher plane of living.

For some of us, that is a mild awakening, while for others it is an awakening into what must feel like a house of horrors. Nevertheless, it is still an awakening. As Dr. Chuck Lofy says throughout his wonderful work on change, "One of the first steps of any journey to change begins by entering the tomb." Without that step, it's like making a journey to a far destination without knowing where you're starting from. It's pulling out that "mental mirror" and taking a look at who you really are on the inside. It's not being afraid of the silence within. It's listening for that distant call from within your soul. It's knowing that whatever you find, it is something to embrace, cradle, and love. And that's when the tomb becomes the womb. That's when you are ready to start thinking about making a great batch of chicken soup for your cluttered life!

The following questions are posed to give you a place to start in looking at your current state of inner equilibrium. They are not meant to be an indictment of any sort, but rather use them as gentle probes. They will be dealt with in greater depth as you read on in the book.

1. Is your happiness centered on "getting what you want" or "wanting what you got"? The point is this: many people don't find happiness because they don't know how to make the most of what they have.
2. Do you hinder your own happiness by constantly striving for the maximum?
3. Are you spending all your time staying consistently busy and on the go, or do you have definite rest stops along the way which you cherish and abide by?

Not long ago, I had a fascinating discussion with a young adult. When we began discussing the prospects of simplifying one's life, she innocently told me, "Most of the people I know probably couldn't even define the term "frugal," let alone remember a time when they tried to be. However, once I tried it, the experience was a lot more pleasant than I expected."

And she is right. It can be. Simplifying your physical and mental lives can be like a warm Chinook wind on a cold winter day. When it comes to your physical domain, take it one room at a time. When it comes to your mental domain, take it thirty minutes a day—one day at a time.

> Most of the luxuries, and many of the so-called comforts of life, are not only not indispensable, but positive hindrances to the elevation of mankind. With respect to luxuries and comforts, the wisest have ever lived a more simple and meagre life than the poor.

—Henry David Thoreau

Reduce the complexity of life by eliminating the needless wants of life, and the labors of life reduce themselves.

—Edwin Way Teale

A few recipes for simplifying your life

• As stated earlier, many people don't find happiness because they don't know how to make the most of what they have. Consequently, they are always trying to get more "stuff" which never seems to bring them satisfaction. Take a few moments and reflect on five things in the past that you worked very hard to acquire. Write them down. Now in looking back at those acquisitions today, do you still find a profound sense of satisfaction with obtaining each of them, or have they been replaced with the search for something newer or bigger? In essence, do they still give the sense of satisfaction that you originally thought they would bring to you? Now make a list of five things you have been wanting to buy. Are they necessities for you, or are they just more stuff?

• Write down a list of five things that truly make you happy and bring you contentment. When you have completed the list, analyze each one of those things and ask yourself two questions. Did I have to spend a lot of money to obtain that item? Second, am I trying to work that item into my life as often as possible?

• Take some time and get to know your neighbors better. Have a neighborhood coffee or wine tasting party where everyone brings their best tasting, least expensive bottle of wine. If you are really creative, see if you can establish a neighborhood talent pool. Maybe you can do some free babysitting in exchange for your neighbor fixing your leaking shower. The bartering business is a great way to save money and develop friends and fellow supporters.

• Here's a great recipe that combines both pride and simplification of one's own life. For the last five years I have picked out a special event I have always looked forward to. For several years it has been watching the Super Bowl. I am an avid football fan and have written a book on it as well. Then, once I have selected the activity or event, I simply give it up. I do without it. Imagine how hard it was to turn to the Discovery channel and bypass the biggest sporting event of the year. But you know what? I survived. In fact, it was one of the most empowering exercises I have ever accomplished. In the end, it wasn't the life or death issue I thought it would be, and I was proud of the fact that I was able to do without something I thought was so precious.

(Picture from the Franklin D. Roosevelt Library, courtesy of the National Archives and Records Administration.)

Choice #3

EMBRACE ADVERSITY

Choice #3

EMBRACE ADVERSITY

Let me embrace thee, sour adversity, for wise men say it is the wisest course.

—William Shakespeare

Too many people who face tough times and tragedies get caught up in the "why me" syndrome. They waste critical time and spiritual energy looking for someone else to blame. At first their anger is their armor, but in time it becomes their prison—a prison cell that can become impossible to escape. Some people say that life is not fair. I say that life is nothing but the time frame in which we are given the ability to live. And like movies, some are epics, and some are short vignettes. In both cases, it's not the length that makes them great—it's the content, and we are the directors.

Many people have a propensity to get so overwhelmed by their difficulties that they fail to put their troubles in perspective. Just last week, I witnessed a friend of mine who spent almost fifteen minutes telling everyone in our coffee group about the sciatic pain he was having in his leg. He went to great lengths to describe all the inconveniences it was causing him, totally oblivious to the man sitting in a wheel chair one table away who had had one leg amputated several months earlier due to his diabetes. One man had accepted his adversity, and the other was engulfed by his. I know a lot of people who think that the current times are about as bad as it can get, but if they knew what their forefathers went through in the early thirties, they would be shocked at how good they still have it today.

Take, for example, Francis Grahn, who was born in 1923 in northern Minnesota to Swedish parents who farmed. The second youngest and only boy of a family with nine children, Francis was six years old when the banks went under and everybody lost their money. His family lost their farm during the Great Depression but continued to rent the farm until they were able to buy it back many years later.

Francis started working on his family's farm when he was five or six years old. His parents would wake him up early in the morning to milk the cows. Francis remembers being so tired that he would fall asleep while milking. His least favorite job was hauling wood all day on Saturdays. He felt like the day would never end.

Francis only went to school for eight years. At age thirteen, he had to quit school to run the family farm after his parents were forced to find work out of state. Even when he attended school, Francis missed over one month during the spring and over one month in the fall to work on the farm. He also was pulled out of school two days a week in the wintertime to haul wood used to heat his family's house. The days he actually attended school, Francis ran home over lunch to feed the family's cows.

The Grahn family, eleven in all, lived in a modest farmhouse. The basement housed the woodstove. The first floor had one bedroom, a living room, and a kitchen. The second floor had one finished bedroom and one unfinished space, which was used for aging flour and as an extra bedroom in the summer. Francis's parents slept in the first-floor bedroom and shared the room with some of their children by hanging a curtain in the middle of the room for privacy. With no indoor plumbing, the family used an outhouse. Francis's parents warned Francis and his sisters to not waste the Montgomery Ward catalog, which they used as toilet paper. The family took a bath once a week in a stand-alone tub filled with water warmed by the woodstove.

Although the Grahn family was poor, they never went hungry. They grew their own food and kept a big garden. They would haul bushels of wheat to a place in town that turned the wheat into flour. The family baked their own bread and picked and canned wild blueberries and everything grown in the garden. They hunted for birds and ate grouse and prairie chickens. When a cow got too sick to produce milk, they would butcher it in the fall and eat it during the winter months. The only thing the family bought at the grocery store was coffee and sugar, and even that was a special treat.

However, to Francis Grahn those were hard but happy years. They were tough times where one's endurance and faith were constantly challenged. They were years filled with one adversity after another, but each was embraced and conquered. When talking about his childhood, eighty-five-year-old Francis never complains. Now compare Francis Grahn's childhood to the kids of today. Kids complain about going to school five days a week. Kids spend hours in front of a television or computer. Kids pout during Christmas if they think they may not get the latest "in thing" for presents. Kids have grown up with an ingrained sense of entitlement. Try to imagine those kids living in Francis Grahn's childhood years.

Some people ask me what I mean by "embracing your adversity." The answer is easier to explain than it is to do. An adversity is anything that can cause a disruption in your life to the point where it can derail your focus in life and your sense of inner contentment. Adversities come in all shapes and sizes—from bad breaks to downers, from mishaps to calamities, from hard times to catastrophes. The key element that makes them adversities is their design. They are all designed to oppose—to attack and disrupt because they are contrary to one's interest or welfare. And the best way to deal with an adversity is to (1) accept it for what it is, (2) move beyond the emotional and mental stress it imposes,

(3) initiate a recovery or coping plan so you can proceed with your life journey without being shackled by it.

Many individuals are very adept at doing just that. Unfortunately, many others are not. They get trapped in the spider's web of the emotional and mental pain. And the longer they spend time in this web, the less chance they have of ever getting out of it. Someone once described it to me this way: "It's like stepping into a quicksand pit. The more you fight it, the more it draws you down into it."

Let me give you an example of how someone was able to embrace his adversity. I shared this true story in an earlier book, but I feel it belongs here as much, if not more. He was a twelve-year-old boy when we met but already had mastered the majestic ability to embrace your adversity and control it instead of letting it control you and your life.

His name was Paul Goodrich, and he lived in the community of Hastings, Nebraska. I called him the "Human Wedge" because he was always trying to separate people from their negative attitudes. He was one of those special few who bring their own sunshine, no matter where they are. If someone was picking on another child on the playground, the Wedge was usually the first person there to break up the fight. If he noticed you were feeling a little down in the dumps, the Wedge was there to cheer you up. When it came to caring and sharing, Paul did it in a fashion most of us give only lip service to.

However, in the fall of my junior year at Hastings College, I got the opportunity to know Paul on a much deeper level. To help pay for my education, I worked as a lab technician at the local hospital. That was the year Paul Goodrich entered the hospital to be diagnosed with leukemia. Back then, that diagnosis was usually a death warrant. Treatment was experimental to say the least. Many of the chemicals that were used were very toxic, and thus the regimen of treatment was constantly changing. The results of his treatment meant that every week or two Paul had to come down to the hospital lab so that we could stick a needle in his arm and draw blood samples for testing how well he was doing in his fight for life. It was not the kind of thing a young boy looks forward to or even handles well. Usually parents have to drag their children in, fighting and kicking every inch of the way.

But that wasn't the case with the Wedge. Every Saturday morning he came into the hospital with a smile on his face. His first statement coming through the door was "Well, is everybody happy today?" When we all answered "Yes," he would immediately raise his arm and reply, "Well, then, you can have my blood today!"

His attitude never varied. Sometimes, he would even roll up his sleeve on his own, wrap that green rubber band around his arm, and start looking for a good vein on his own. Not once in over two years did I ever see him entrapped in the negative emotions that could pull him down.

One Saturday, many months later, he came in for his appointment, saying as always, "Well, is everybody happy today?" Everybody responded with a big "Yes" except for me. I was sitting on one of the lab stools, doing a microscopic examination of a blood sample and said nothing.

Noticing my silence, he said, "I didn't hear you say yes, David. Do you have a smile for me this morning?"

I simply replied, "Paul, I had a rather bad night last night and, quite frankly, don't feel like smiling for anyone today." In retrospect, I can't believe that I talked that way to a young boy who was fighting for his life.

Without any hesitation, Paul shot back, "David, if you want my blood today, you are going to have to give me a smile." With those words, the Wedge leaped into the air, threw his arms around my neck in an arm lock, nearly tipping over the microscope and shouted to the rest of the people in the lab, "I'm going to hold onto David until I squeeze a smile out of him. I can't see his face, so someone tell me when he gives in and smiles." And that's exactly what he did. He held me with every ounce of his strength until I gave in and smiled.

Time passed and later that year I took some time off from the lab. When I returned, the next weekend, Paul Goodrich came through the door as usual. "Well, is everybody happy today?" As I turned to say "Yes" and give him a big smile, I almost went into a state of shock. Since I had last seen him, Paul had lost a lot of weight and body tone. His face was sunken, and his skin was ashen. I could see in his eyes he had lost the battle, and I sensed that he knew it as well.

Never in my life have I desired to do something for someone as much as I wanted to do something for him at that moment. I wanted to give to him what he so relentlessly gave to others. But I didn't know what to do or say. As I sat down and wrapped the rubber band around his arm for what I felt was the thousandth time, I had a feeble thought. Thinking it might cheer him up a little, I asked, "Paul, if you could have anything in the world right now, what would it be?"

"Anything?" he replied.

"Absolutely anything," I said.

Without any hesitation, he looked at me and said, "I already know what I want."

Surprised by his quick response, I asked him what it would be.

"David," he said, "if I could have anything in the world right now, it would be that my mom and my dad might be happy when I am no longer here . . . for I'm not going to be here much longer, and I am not sure they are ready for that."

Before me sat a young boy less than a month away from death's door, and even then he still wanted to give before he would ever think of receiving. He made chicken soup for everyone and served his cuisine in a style very few have dared to try. And he was just a boy.

If you can internalize the selfless spirit of Paul Goodrich into your life, you can throw the rest of this book away, for you will then have the power and the skills to change not only your life but the rest of the world as well. And what a wonderful world that would be.

How did Paul Goodrich do it? He simply embraced the adversity that stormed into his life at such an early age. He had every right to be angry, but he didn't fall into that quicksand pit. Instead, he accepted it, and then he put his plan into action. He transformed his adversity into a companion to help himself and others. I believe he somehow instinctively realized that the length of life pales in comparison to the quality of life, and Paul Goodrich was not going to allow his cancer to destroy his faith. He reminds me of what the poet John Greenleaf Whittier once wrote, "We need love's tender lessons taught—as only weakness can. God hath his small interpreters,—the child must teach the man."

I doubt if any person reading this book does not know of someone who is facing some sort of hardship or misfortune right now. Jobs are dropping off the landscape like leaves in a fall windstorm. Thousands are being forced to give up their homes and file for bankruptcy. Ruptured retirement plans are decimating the dreams of people all across this country. Most of these maladies cannot be avoided, but recovery will never be achieved if we remain victims of the negative force that disrupted our lives. Just take a drive through New Orleans and you will see what I mean. Many victims never tried to rebuild because they remained victims of the tragedy. Others shed their tears, took time to mourn their loss, and then took charge of their lives again.

A few years ago, I was giving a speech at a convention being held in Riverside, Wyoming. Due to a number of complications, I and another speaker were required to rent a car and drive about two hundred miles to Cheyenne in order to make a flight connection. He held the map, and I drove the car. We headed east on a single lane highway he chose and drove for over an hour when suddenly the road came to a dead end. It was a road specifically built to a distant mining company, but we didn't realize it. Needless to say, we had to turn around and drive some eighty miles back to catch the right highway. Both of us were upset because our ability to catch our connecting flight was now in severe jeopardy.

After about ten minutes of shedding my misery, I put it behind me and focused on what shortcuts we might now find to get us there in time. Unfortunately, my friend couldn't do the same. For the next four hours, he stewed, complained, and occasionally slammed his fist against the dashboard. He cursed the mining company for building a dead-end road, the state highway commission for not clearly marking the road, and about everyone else he could think of. He eventually even suggested that I should have been more alert to the potential of our mistake. It was a journey of constant misery, and I am glad to say I have never heard from him again. Yes, I was upset and disappointed and vented my frustration. But when that was done, I was able to move on. It was over, and there was nothing we could do to change our little adversity. I let it go and made the course corrections needed to get back on track. He couldn't. I know it sounds simplistic, but letting go of your troubles is a key ingredient for making your own chicken soup in troubled times.

I have two friends that reflect the difference between embracing and not embracing one's adversities. One friend lost his job about ten months ago. He was angry. He too blamed about everyone he could think of. He was, and still is today, a classic victim. Oh, he looked around for another job, but he refused to look for one that didn't match his previous position. And when he got an occasional interview, he went to that interview not as an eager applicant ready to demonstrate his potential but rather as a victim of the past employer who had let him go. Today, he sits at home watching soap operas and waits for a miracle to take place. Several other less-paying jobs have been offered to him, but he has turned them all down. And in the process he has lost his wife and his life savings, and is now in the process of moving from a $200,000 home into a dilapidated trailer he managed to buy for about $15,000.

My other friend suddenly lost his job as well. He was a line manager of a motor home plant and was making a very good salary. He went through a period of mourning, but after embracing his adversity, he let it go. When he started looking for new employment, he took a serious look at everything available. After several weeks, he found what he later stated was "just what I wanted." When I asked him to explain what he meant, he told me, "It isn't the ideal job in the world, but it will give me an opportunity to meet my current needs and, more importantly, an opportunity to retool my talents and get ready for the economic recovery when it arrives."

Both of these friends have a lot of things in common when it comes to other factors in their lives. They are about the same age. They are both intelligent, educated individuals. They both have a strong track record of past successes. The big factor that has made all the difference in their lives is simply this: one was able to embrace his adversity and the other was overwhelmed. Embracing one's adversity is the critical first step we all have to take before we can move beyond our struggles and reclaim our lives. Ironically, only by embracing it can we then break free from it.

> I have heard there are troubles of more than one kind. Some come from ahead and some come from behind. But I've bought a big bat. I'm all ready you see. Now my troubles are going to have troubles with me!

—Dr. Seuss

A few recipes for embracing adversities

• Think back about your last week or two. List three instances when something didn't go the way you had planned.

1.
2.
3.

Now go back over the above list and circle each instance where you didn't point the finger of blame at someone else. Make a promise to yourself to get through the next week without blaming someone else when something doesn't go right or doesn't get done.

• Write a personal mission statement of how you will embrace adversities in the future. Make it a three- or four-step formula. When completed, frame one version and hang it on the wall at your normal workstation. Then give copies to a few of your closest friends with instructions to them to confront you if you ever fail to meet that mission.

(Picture from the Franklin D. Roosevelt Library, courtesy of the
National Archives and Records Administration.)

Choice #4

CHANGE YOUR ATTITUDE

Choice #4

CHANGE YOUR ATTITUDE

When written in Chinese, the word "crisis" is composed of two characters—one represents danger and the other represents opportunity.

—John F. Kennedy

All the adversity I've had in my life, all my troubles and obstacles, have strengthened me . . . You may not realize it when it happens, but a kick in the teeth may be the best thing in the world for you.

—Walt Disney

I love people who wake up each day and say, "Good morning, Lord." However, today there are just too many people who get up and say, "Good Lord, morning."

It's much like the message I tried to convey when I wrote the poem, "The Rose Versus the Thorn".

The day you stop living today,
Is the day you start preparing to die.
And the day you stop smelling the roses,
Is the hour your soul learns to cry.

Oh, I know your troubles are many,
And inside the sorrow may be great,
But the damage it does to your spirit,
Is something only you regulate.

There are many whose actions disturb us,
There's even more we can find to blame,
But the force of the blow to the spirit,
Is something only you can inflame.

So when you tell me your troubles,
And how life has been so unfair.
Please understand that I'll listen,
But I won't be drawn into that snare.

And when you finish your tale of injustice,
Having emptied your bucket of sorrow,
I'll simply ask if you intend to forget them,
Or will they be back in your bucket tomorrow?

Will you let the damage of yesterday,
Re-inflict damage upon you today?
Will you allow your anger to become cancerous,
And continue to fester and decay?

Or will you instead shed your tears of sorrow,
Then get back up upon your feet;
Thanking God for giving you the power,
To claim victory instead of defeat?

Oh, life is always going to have problems,
And there are far too many who live it in scorn,
But God promises to all who will listen,
If you can smell the roses you can cradle the thorn.

In times of trials and tribulations, what do you set your sights on? Do you become entrapped by the negative side of life, or is your focus on the positive? An old friend of mine used to say, "There are just too many people in this country who look like they have been weaned on a pickle—they're all puckered up about everything." The great playwright George Bernard Shaw once said, "People are always blaming their circumstances for what they are. I don't believe in circumstances. The people who get on in this world are the people who get up and look for the circumstances they want, and, if they can't find them, make them."

It's very easy to see the dark side of life when you see yourself as a victim, and once you embrace a negative vision about life, you'll become its ambassador. I know individuals who start out each day with a "Good Lord" attitude. They get up and immediately have to give themselves a caffeine or cigarette fix. Then they turn on the television to watch the latest tragedy in Iraq, the stock market decline in the Far East, the latest sensational murder, or a thousand other negative items to focus on. Next comes the local newspaper and its propensity for the negative drift. When they head to work, they drive like gladiators waiting for the next idiot to cut in on their lane of traffic. When they get to work and have a department meeting to attend, they go to the meeting prepared to do battle—to defend their turf. The list could go on and on. Too many people approach their work with a "them against me" attitude. And then they try to "fix" their lives through a host of unhealthy addictions. Is this the American way of life you want to live?

If you relate to the above description, let me ask you this question: would you allow me to come into your house each morning with a five-gallon bucket of fresh cow manure and dump it over your head, saying, "Now go out there and make a positive difference in someone else's life." I doubt it; but that's exactly what so many of us do to ourselves each day, emotionally, spiritually, and mentally, simply by what we choose to focus our vision on each morning as we wake up. We inadvertently choose a negative vision of life instead of a positive approach. When that happens, we invite the negative elements in life to take control of our attitude about life, and we do it day after day after day.

I remember hearing a statement made by a speaker many years ago that has echoed in my mind ever since. He said, "Everything happens for a reason and a purpose—and it serves us." That requires faith, faith in a lot of things, but when it comes to rising above adversity, the most important is faith in yourself. In over twenty years of working with individuals all over this country, the only individuals I have observed who were not able to get back on their feet and dance again were those who didn't believe. They became victims of their circumstances instead of commanders.

Let me give you several examples of individuals who perfected the power of turning negatives into positives. As I read this list of adversities encountered by this first individual, compare his struggles to those you may be facing.

•He was born into a poor immigrant family in 1767. They had just enough money to make a down payment on a small farm, but they lost that farm when his father died just five days after he was born.

• Shortly after his father's death, his mother and his two older brothers were forced to move into a destitute section of the state where they lived in total poverty.

• When the Revolution broke out, his oldest brother enlisted and was killed a month later.

• At the age of thirteen, he and his other brother enlisted as well and were both captured and imprisoned.

• When this young boy refused to clean a Tory's boots, the officer swung his sword at him, wounding him and causing a partial paralysis in his arm.

• When his brother refused as well, he too was slashed deeply across the head and neck.

• Both continued to suffer from their undressed wounds and shortly after that were infected with smallpox.

• A month later there was a prisoner exchange, and their mother was allowed to take them home.

• At fourteen, barefoot, half naked, sick with smallpox, and starving, he walked forty miles on foot in chilling temperatures and heavy rain so that his mother and brother might ride.

• Two days later, his brother died. His own life hung by a thread.

• Then, just as he began to recover, his mother suddenly took ill and died.

• At the age of fifteen he was left alone, penniless, and without a single friend or relative to turn to.

Tell me this, do you know of anyone in your life who has more strikes against them than this boy had by the age of fifteen? Can you think of anyone who would have greater justification to surrender to adversity? Anyone who had a better right to say, "I got cheated." "I quit." "I'm beaten." "I can't go on." "Life is not fair."

Well, he didn't surrender because he had the courage to embrace adversity. Regardless of the storms of grief and agony he would have to endure, there was a voice within him that said, "You can do it." He diligently kept a positive attitude about his future, and despite all of those tragedies, he rose above them all.

Three years later, he entered law school in North Carolina. When he graduated, he got his first appointment as a lawyer at the age of twenty-one. And not many years after that, he took the oath to become the seventh president of the United States of America. For that boy was none other than Andrew Jackson.

Let's move forward about 135 years and look at a more modern example. In 1965, a thirty-eight-year-old woman was trying to start her life over after going through a tough divorce. Suddenly being a single parent from New Orleans, she was looking to start a new business so she could put her two sons through college.

Finally she spotted an ad for a restaurant and thought, "I wonder if I could do that?" She thought about it and finally found the courage to seize the possibilities. So, without any experience in the restaurant business, she mortgaged her home and bought a restaurant where the past six owners had failed to succeed.

Ruth Fertel began to do whatever she needed to do to make her business a success. She learned all there was to learn about hosting, waitressing, cooking, bartending, and even butchering thirty-pound loins of beef. And for a woman who was only five foot, two inches and weighed only one hundred and ten pounds, that was not an easy task. She worked seven days a week, serving thirty five steaks a day for five dollars each. But she made a profit, and soon other people were admiring both her audacity to achieve and the taste of a great steak.

Then came the garbage truck of life in the form of Hurricane Betsy. It devastated New Orleans, knocking out power to her large cooler filled with steaks at her restaurant. But her broilers still worked, so she cooked free steak meals for many disaster victims and relief workers. That sacrifice came back to reward her. She embraced her adversity, and with her positive attitude, she didn't let it control her desire to achieve. After surviving her loss, she began rebuilding her business once more. Her generosity was noted by many individuals who returned as new customers once she was back on her feet.

But she didn't stop there. With her background in science and the tenacity of a bulldog, she decided to make her business even better than what it was before. She wanted to cook the best USDA prime, corn-fed steak available anywhere in America. That was when she invented and patented a grill that would sear her steaks at 1,800 degrees! And when they were done, they were placed on a plate hot enough to keep them perfect until the last piece was swallowed.

It was that same audacity to seize possibilities that led her to launch her first franchise in 1977. Today there are well over one hundred Ruth's Chris Steakhouse restaurants in the United States and four foreign countries, and it is the largest chain in the world in the luxury steak market.

There is one other key I have discovered in these last twenty years of watching people struggle to overcome hard times. It is reflected in every story I find and every person I have met who maintains a positive, proactive attitude about adversities. This is it: when those moments of adversity strike, within a very brief period of time, they are dismissed. They are no longer a factor in the game plan for tomorrow. They absorb any lessons to be learned and then move on. They might lose a battle, but they remain committed to win the war! How is that possible? It is possible because they choose a positive approach over a negative one.

Now I'm not going to promise that if you change every negative into a positive, you will eventually become president of the United States or a millionaire. That's not going to happen for most of us. However, I will promise you this: if you strive to empower yourself with a will to make the most of every negative situation, you will find contentment and peace of mind, regardless of the circumstance.

The ornithologist Audubon once told of how he was able to turn a negative into a positive.

"It was an accident," he said, "which happened to two hundred of my original drawings, nearly put a stop to my researches in ornithology, the study of birds. I left the village of Henderson, Kentucky, where I resided for several years, to proceed to Philadelphia on business. I looked to my drawings before my departure, placed them carefully in a wooden box, and gave them to a relative, with instructions to see that no injury should happen to them. My absence was of several months, and when I returned, after having enjoyed the pleasures of home for a few days, I inquired after my box, and what I pleased to call my treasure.

"The box was produced and opened; but, reader, feel for me; a pair of Norway rats had taken possession of the whole, and reared a young family among the gnawed bits of paper, which, but a month previous, represented nearly a thousand inhabitants of the air! The burning heat, which instantly rushed through my brain, was too great to be endured without affecting my whole nervous system. I slept for several nights, and then regaining my constitution, I took my gun, my notebook, and my pencils, and went forth to the woods as gaily as if nothing had happened. I felt pleased that I might make better drawings than before; and, ere a period not exceeding three years had elapsed, my portfolio was again filled." He too embraced his adversity and then released its grip on his life.

There's an old story told about a man who asked his friend Fred how things were going for him. His friend answered, "Oh, pretty good under the circumstances." Then his friend asked him how his job was going, and Fred replied, "Oh, pretty good under the circumstances." Finally the friend asked how his family was doing, and once again Fred answered, "Oh, pretty good under the circumstances."

Unfortunately, too many people live "under the circumstances." They become entrapped in the negative; and like a spider's web, it keeps pulling them in, tighter and tighter. If that's beginning to happen to you, the best way out of the web is to break one strand at a time. Make a list of all the elements that impact your life. Your list should include your health, your spiritual life, your career or occupation, your family, your love relationship, your social life, and other elements. Then take a close look at each one, and ask yourself if you are living under the circumstances of that element. If your answer is yes, then make out a plan for improvement and focus on making it a positive element of your life. Focus on only one element at a time. Don't try to address all of them at once. If you make a focused commitment to break that strand, I promise you it will make an incredible difference.

Zig Ziglar, who I like to refer to as the Paul Harvey of motivational speakers, used to tell his audiences that the most important five minutes of your day were the first five minutes after waking up. Those moments will set the tone for the rest of the day, and we are in complete control of the attitude we set. So instead of turning on the television, turn on a CD that consistently lifts up your spirit or even makes you sing along. Instead of reading the newspaper, start off by reading something humorous or inspirational. And instead of taking the fast lane to work, start out a few minutes earlier and drive through a park or a quiet boulevard. As an old saying goes, "Count the garden by the flowers, never by the leaves that fall. Count your life with smiles and not the tears that fall."

A healthy attitude is like the thunder in a spring shower. It is a part of the core, not the veneer. It is not a coat of armor that you retrieve from your war chest before the battle begins. It is part of one's internal armor, housed within and worn at all times, through all things. A positive attitude cannot be swept away with the tide of events. It is constantly at work to find meaning and purpose in all events, throughout all of life's encounters.

So choose an attitude that brings beauty and hope into your heart, and employ that vision in the first moments of your wakening. Avoid the anchor of negativity others relentlessly cast over the side of their boat and then wonder why they can't make it out of the bay of remorse. And when the storms of life descend, you will be the first to see the rainbow that follows.

> Develop success from failures. Discouragement and failure are two of the surest stepping stones to success.
>
> —Dale Carnegie

> Failure is often that early morning hour of darkness which precedes the dawning of the day of success.
>
> —Leigh Mitchell Hodges

A few recipes for keeping a positive attitude

• Take someone special for a leisurely walk or bike ride around an area lake, a sleepy countryside, or a serene state park late in the afternoon or evening. Have no definite destination, and if the stars are out and the weather permits, do a little star gazing. Each time you go for a walk, come up with a list of at least ten things that you appreciate and are thankful for.

• Start a "Friends" or "Neighborhood" library. Simply have people put together a list of ten attitude enrichment books, CDs, or DVDs they have collected and are willing to share. Have one person combine the list and make copies. You might even have them note their recommendations along with the titles. Why buy a book when you could borrow it?

• Buy a copy of your favorite newspaper and a large, black magic marker. Start on page one of the main section, and cross out every negative article you see. This should include negative economic news, crimes, and other articles with a negative drift. Hopefully, you won't run your magic marker dry in the process. Now reflect on just how much bad news you are letting into your thoughts and the damage it can do to your positive attitude. And while you're at it, do the same with a TV Guide.

• Make a list of the three things you complain about most. Put a rubber band around your wrist, and every time you find yourself slipping into that "gritch" bucket, snap the rubber band hard and lift your mind to a higher level of thought.

(Picture from the Franklin D. Roosevelt Library, courtesy of the
National Archives and Records Administration.)

Choice #5

BREAK THE SILENCE

Choice #5

BREAK THE SILENCE

Sharing is loving.

—Unknown

The sorrows which hurt the most—
are the ones you hide within.

—Unknown

In the seventies, I served as an assistant administrator of a large hospital in Lincoln, Nebraska. A major service area of our institution was in the field of oncology. One day I was speaking with our hospital chaplain about how hard it must be on him to keep his own spirits up while dealing with tragedy after tragedy. When I asked him what one of the most difficult challenges of the job was, he said it was getting families to the point of being comfortable talking about the disease. He said, "The word cancer is like a dirty word that no one wants to utter. So they avoid bringing it up in fear they will depress the patient even more." He said visitors would come and go without bringing the subject up. Consequently, the silence surrounding the disease was really hard for the patients to deal with. The silence often hurt the most.

In the mideighties, I became involved with counseling families during the farm crisis that was taking place across America. During those hard times, I discovered one poignant factor which I consistently found in troubled families. It was the silence that affected families. It separated husbands from their wives and even their children. And for some, it was devastating! Proud fathers desperately avoided bringing up the uncertainty they faced, but in their effort to spare their families, they did even more damage. I met wives who had been married for years who were thinking about leaving because they had been shut out. Some did. I interviewed young teenagers who contemplated running away from home to help reduce the financial stress they knew was there but no one talked about. Unfortunately, some did. The silence hurt the most.

In troubled times, silence hurts. Silence alienates. Silence feeds doubts. Silence destroys relationships. And yet it's one of the most common paths individuals follow when their lives or their careers appear to be crumbling. It's as if they don't believe other members of their family have even a hint of what is going on. However, in reality, they do. And in the silence, their imagination tends to stretch the fear beyond the actuality of the plight.

Surviving tough times is best accomplished as a team effort. I could give you countless examples of the positive effect sharing can produce. I know of an eight-year-old girl who, just last year, sensing her mother's hardship, emptied her piggy bank and secretly put the money in her single-parent mother's purse to help out. Recently, a college student sent the money she was making in a part-time job on campus home to her parents with a note saying she just wanted to help them out and could live without the money. One woman, who after finally getting her husband to open up about his failing construction business, became an intimate partner in helping him refocus his outlook. She helped him develop a successful remodeling business instead of just doing new construction. Her ingenious approach was to make the client part of the remodeling team so he could teach his clients about carpentry skills as they helped him do the job. The customers loved it, and in the process, the husband and wife's relationship grew stronger than ever before.

I like to remind couples under the pressure of troubled times to think back and remember one of the happiest times of their lives together. In over 75 percent of the responses, they will recall the first months or years of their marriage. For many, including my wife and myself, it was a time of just struggling to get started; but we did it as a team. Back then, I had just graduated from college and had my first teaching contract for $7,370. If you had mentioned the term "discretionary income" to my wife and me, we wouldn't have had the slightest idea of what that meant. We didn't know that you couldn't be happy and nearly broke at the same time.

We were happy because it didn't take much to make us happy. A great social outing was when we got together with several other couples on Friday night and ate some macaroni and cheese with hot dogs on the side. Then, after we pooled our money to buy a couple of six-packs of the cheapest beer available, we would settle in for a night of playing cards or Monopoly. We were all on the same team. Today, those are still some of our fondest memories in forty years of being married.

A great way to break the bondage of silence is to bring everybody in your inner circle of friends or family together once a week and conduct what I call "The Week's Best and The Worst." We started it with our children by accident when they were very young. Eventually, it became a time together we all looked forward to. We would go around the room—each person starting out sharing the best thing that had happened to them that week. It could be getting a B on a school test for the kids and a pat on the back from my boss for me. When everyone had completed the best of the week we went around the room again, sharing something that was disappointing or hurtful.

At first, there was a reluctance to share a negative that really hurt, but as time passed I think we all looked forward to this portion the most. It felt good to unburden. It helped even more when others would give each other comfort or even suggestions. And I believe we all learned it is far, far better to share our pain and disappointment rather than to carry it around, hoping no one will discover it. It really works well with friends too. Make it part of your TGIF routine. Do a BYO at your house or apartment with some close friends and have the courage to share this idea. Just tell them that some crazy, old writer challenged you to give it a try. You won't be sorry you did.

Let me put it this way: if you were on a lifeboat in the middle of a troubled sea with six other people, would you just sit there and ignore everyone else, or would you try to pull everyone together and face the challenge as a team? Don't underestimate the ability of those you love and care for. It might not be their job that's in jeopardy, but they are there on that lifeboat with you. Bring them into your troubled times. Ask for their contributions. Break the silence, share your troubles, ask for help, and allow them to be part of your team.

> Deep in my heart I'm concealing things that I'm longing to say. Scared to confess what I'm feeling-frightened you'll slip away.

—Evita the Musical

> I hid my burden inside,
> And nearly tore myself apart.
> Then I shared my troubles with a friend,
> And in so doing, healed my broken heart.

—Unknown

A few recipes for breaking the silence

• Handwrite a letter to a friend and share a message of hope about the future. Let them know you are available if they ever need to talk to someone.

• Go to iTunes and pull up Bill Withers's song, "Lean on Me." Make a copy of his incredible tune and send it along with a personal note to a friend you sense might benefit from your personal contact. Here are the lyrics:

Sometimes in our lives we all have pain
We all have sorrow
But if we are wise
We know that there's always tomorrow

Lean on me, when you're not strong
And I'll be your friend
I'll help you carry on
For it won't be long
'Til I'm gonna need
Somebody to lean on

Please swallow your pride
If I have things you need to borrow
For no one can fill those of your needs
That you won't let show

You just call on me, brother, when you need a hand
We all need somebody to lean on
I just might have a problem that you'll understand
We all need somebody to lean on

Lean on me, when you're not strong
And I'll be your friend
I'll help you carry on
For it won't be long
'Til I'm gonna need
Somebody to lean on

You just call on me, brother, when you need a hand
We all need somebody to lean on
I just might have a problem that you'll understand
We all need somebody to lean on

If there is a load you have to bear
That you can't carry
I'm right up the road
I'll share your load
If you just call me

Call me, if you need a friend
Call me, if you ever need a friend
Call me, call me, call me . . .

• Get creative and form your own support group of close friends you know who are trying to find solutions to their economic woes. Give it a name like "Frugal Friends." Meet together one night every other week for the evening, and make it a brown bag dinner. Give a door prize to the person or couple who comes up with the least expensive but tasteful meal. Then, after a little socialization, have each person share at least one way they were able to save a little money since you last met. You will be amazed at the fun and results you'll have.

(Picture from the Franklin D. Roosevelt Library, courtesy of the National Archives and Records Administration.)

Choice #6

USE FAITH TO CONQUER DOUBT

Choice #6

USE FAITH TO CONQUER DOUBT

Faith is a bird that feels dawn breaking and sings while it's still dark.

—Old Scandinavian Saying

All I have seen teaches me to trust the Creator for all I have not seen.

—Ralph Waldo Emerson

There is one final element reflected in Mr. Wall's little note that I believe is an imperative to making a great batch of chicken soup for troubled times. Without it, one can survive, but with it, one can excel. I believe it is the one ingredient that can change an average batch of chicken soup into an inimitable cuisine of potential. That ingredient is faith.

It's been said that faith is staying focused on the positive and being grateful for what you have. Faith is trusting that the right answer to a problem will come to you; it's waiting patiently until things get resolved and knowing that prayer can be answered in many ways. Helen Keller said it this way: "Faith is the strength by which a shattered world shall emerge into the light."

Today, many people feel like their world has been shattered. They have lost their jobs, their homes, their retirement savings, and much, much more. But I believe that faith is the one precious knot at the end of the rope which we must hold onto when our world is crumbling beneath us.

Now I'm not going to present anyone with a religious dissertation on faith. Although it is a very big part of my life, there are many aspects of organized religions that make me both uncomfortable and angry. One only needs to look at the number of people who have been killed in the name of religion to see what I mean. Since before the Great Crusades, mankind has been trying to force its religion upon someone else. And I have no problems with denominations and their traditions. They give us a tent under which we can come together and celebrate our faith. Unfortunately, where most people are driven away from faith is when they become exposed to the prejudice espoused by those denominations. I have always said it this way: I don't care what you call Him—just as long as you call on Him.

When I was very young, I heard a poem by James Henry Leigh Hunt which absolutely captured my soul and has been the reflection of my faith ever since. He wrote it around 1838 and gave it the title "Abou Ben Adhem." It goes this way:

> Abou Ben Adhem (may his tribe increase!)
> Awoke one night from a deep dream of peace,
> And saw, within the moonlight in his room,
> Making it rich, and like a lily in bloom,
> An angel writing in a book of gold:
>
> Exceeding peace had made Ben Adhem bold,
> And to the Presence in the room he said,
> "What writest thou?"
> The vision raised its head,
> And with a look made of all sweet accord,
> Answered, "The names of those who love the Lord."
>
> "And is mine one?" said Abou.

"Nay, not so," replied the angel.
Abou spoke more low,
But cheerily still; and said, "I pray thee, then,
Write me as one that loves his fellow men."

The angel wrote, and vanished.
The next night it came again with a great wakening light,
And showed the names whom love of God had blest,
And lo! Ben Adhem's name led all the rest.

James Leigh Hunt

In all my years, in over 2,500 speaking engagements and the thousands of people I have met from Alaska to Cairo, Egypt during that time, I have always found two consistent groups of people that stand out the most. The first group consists of individuals who weave their faith into the very fabric of their daily lives. I don't mean that they go about and preach their gospel to everybody. Rather, they simply live through faith in all circumstances. Yes, they get disgruntled like everyone else. Yes, they get angry when disappointment comes into their lives. Yes, they have their moments where doubt sweeps over them, but they always seem to have the ability to pop back up to the surface like a bobber on the end of a fishing line. And when I ask them what the critical ingredient to their buoyancy is—they always mention their faith.

The second group includes those who don't have a sense of faith in anything greater than themselves. These are the ones who *always* come forward at the end of my presentations with one question on their mind. "Where do I need to go; what do I need to do to find the sense of internal peace I refer to?" You see, the BMW didn't do it. The new job title didn't give it to them. And the $500,000 home still leaves them with a void inside. It's much like the old saying, "Those who have faith need no explanation; for those who have no faith, no explanation is possible."

Duke University once did a study of truly contented people. They examined hundreds of individuals who were able to maintain a great sense of inner equilibrium. And when all of the key elements were listed, a belief in something greater than oneself was right there at the top of the list. Like Albert Einstein once said, "There are only two ways to live . . . one is as though nothing is a miracle . . . the other is as if everything is." Faith keeps us focused on the positive. It bridges the chasm between our failures and our successes. It keeps us in the game even when the score is not in our favor. It allows us patience when chaos and uncertainty dominate our domain. And it gives us both the power and the humility to pray for greater guidance and resolve to conquer those tough moments.

When we embrace that foundational faith, it then allows us to generate faith in our own lives, in stronger relationships with others, in challenges we face, and in many other different ways as well. In tough times, I believe that a strong sense of faith is like the famed Energizer bunny that keeps on going. It is the driving force that helps us penetrate those moments when we want to quit and give up. I have a friend named Dr. Jerry Winter who is a long-distance marathon runner who says it's faith that he embraces as he approaches what he calls "the runner's wall." It's a point in the race when every part of the body is telling runners to back off and quit. Mentally and physically, they are about to collapse. Some do, but the ones who have faith in themselves know that the wall is just a barrier to break through, and once you do, success is assured. He said, "It's not the distance that's hardest to achieve. It's the will to go the distance, and that takes faith."

Here's a key sentence to remember: "faith," produces endurance, and in these challenging days, endurance is the name of the game. The classical Roman poet Virgil once said, "Come what may, all bad fortune is to be conquered by endurance." William Barclay, the author and Biblical scholar, said, "Endurance is not just the ability to bear a hard thing, but to turn it into glory." And the great Scottish writer Thomas Carlyle once wrote, "Endurance is patience concentrated."

Tough times demand endurance because during tough times there are many things which are beyond our control. Right now as I am writing this book, I would like to put about 75 percent of America's bankers, politicians, financial managers, and corporate executives in jail. However, that's not within my realm of power. I would like to magically create a stock market rally which would help people recover the dramatic losses they have experienced. And I would really like to chain individuals like Bernard Madoff to the dog house sitting in my backyard. But that too is beyond my control.

What I can do is endure. I can use the focused endurance I have, which my faith provides, and strive, endeavor, and paddle my way through the troubled waters until I reach calmer seas. Without faith, it often becomes an insurmountable task for many.

Erma Bombeck, the beloved American humorist, used to advise people who face challenges to make out what she called "The Horror Floor." It was a simple list of all the things that could go wrong while you were trying to succeed at something. No positives should be listed—just the negatives. When you complete your list, she said to look it over one more time and then answer one simple question: "So what?" Think about that for a few minutes. Her contention was that once you have looked at the worst possibilities, you will realize that life will go on. It will be OK. Things will get better. And once you have achieved that resolution, the battle will be won.

I think the philosophy behind that exercise is the fact that when we face our fears—when we look through all the shadows of doubt and despair—we can then see the light and find the faith to endure. To reach this level of living will not take place overnight. You can't simply snap your fingers and have faith come into your life. But you can take it one day and one struggle at a time. Choose one spirit-draining element you currently face, and once you have embraced all elements of it, make the focused commitment to rise above it. You see, faith is a powerful, prevailing, and commanding force within all of us. It just takes the resolve to claim it. And while you are at it, if you've given up on going to a religious service, give it another chance. Try a different denomination or sect if you've been disappointed with where you attended earlier. It just might be one of the best single hours you have ever invested.

To be hopeful in bad times is not just foolishly romantic. It is based on the fact that human history is a history not only of cruelty but also of compassion, sacrifice, courage, kindness. What we choose to emphasize in this complex history will determine our lives. If we see only the worst, it destroys our capacity to do something. If we remember those times and places—and there are so many—where people have behaved magnificently, this gives us the energy to act, and at least the possibility of sending this spinning top of a world in a different direction. And if we do act, in however small a way, we don't have to wait for some grand utopian future. The future is an infinite succession of presents, and to live now as we think human beings should live, in defiance of all that is bad around us, is itself a marvelous victory.

—Howard Zinn

There is no gain except by loss;
There is no life except by death;
There is no vision except by faith.
—Walter Chalmers Smith

A few recipes for building your faith

• After you have read the following poem at least twice, ask yourself if you could be a little bit more like this author next week.

MY CUP HAS OVERFLOWED

I've never made a fortune,
And it's probably too late now
But I don't worry about that much
I'm happy anyhow.
And as I go along life's journey
I'm reaping better than I sowed,
I'm drinking from the saucer
Cause my cup has overflowed.

I ain't got a lot of riches
Sometimes the going's tough,
But I got a family that loves me
That makes me rich enough.
I just thank God for His blessings
And the mercy He's bestowed,
I'm drinking from my saucer
Cause my cup has overflowed.

Oh, I remember times when things went wrong
My faith got a little bit thin,
But then all at once the dark clouds broke
And that old sun peaked thru again.
So Lord help me not to gripe
About the tough rows that I've hoed
I'm drinking from my saucer
Cause my cup has overflowed.

And if God gives me strength and courage
When the ways grow steep and rough
I'll not ask for other blessings
I'm already blessed enough.
And may I never be too busy
To help another bear his load
Then I'll keep drinking from my saucer
Cause my cup has overflowed.

Anonymous

• Pick out someone you know and think of a way you can do something special for them. Once you have decided what you are going to do, do it, but don't get caught.

• Buy or check out a copy of Canfield and Hansen's book, *Chicken Soup for the Christian Soul*. Don't worry, you're not going to get hit with a bolt of lightning from the sky. Turn to chapter 4, "On Faith," and read what a few other people have to say.

(Picture from the Franklin D. Roosevelt Library, courtesy of the
National Archives and Records Administration.)

Chapter 7

WHERE DO WE GO FROM HERE?

Chapter 7

WHERE DO WE GO FROM HERE?

Happy is he who still loves something he loved in the nursery: He has not been broken in two by time; he is not two men, but one, and he has saved not only his soul but his life.

—G. K. Chesterton

I will never forget a trip our family took a number of years ago with our two teenage children to Cancun, Mexico. One of the highlights of the trip was a bus tour to the Chichen Itza pyramids on the Yucatan Peninsula. The journey took several hours to get there, but it gave us a wonderful opportunity to see the more rural parts of the countryside.

One of the things that repeatedly caught our attention was when we would pass by little hamlets beside the highway. The scene was always the same. We would see these small cabana-style family homes nestled in the trees. Many of them didn't have glass in their windows. Their designs were very simple, and from where we observed them, their sizes were limited to one or two rooms.

Outside you could usually find children playing and at least one pig tied to a rope and anchored to a tree. This was repeated time after time; and I, like most everyone else on the bus, silently said to myself, "I'm glad I live in America and don't have to put up with this." And then all of us received a great lesson. Pulling up to a rest stop, the tour guide stood up in the front of the bus, picked up the microphone, and said this: "People, I have been observing you for the last hour or so. I have seen the look on your faces as we passed many of the little family abodes. However, I want you to know one thing. Don't feel sorry for these people. They are some of the happiest people on the face of the earth. Their families are extremely close-knit. They are healthy people. Each child has at least two outfits to wear, and one of them is always clean. They don't have drug problems out here. They don't have other abuse problems either. Violence is almost nonexistent. They live in extremely warm and friendly communities and have a very strong sense of faith. In fact, I'll bet if you compare their lives to yours, you would end up feeling sorry for yourselves and not them."

That moment in time will stay with me forever. Why? Because he was right. Now I'm not suggesting we should all strive to obtain abject poverty as our standard of living to find peace of mind. What I am suggesting is that we don't need "stuff" to be happy. We don't need exorbitant homes or expensive cars or executive titles to find our self-esteem. In fact, many of those things only draw us deeper and deeper into the stress of keeping what we have and getting even more tomorrow. I have always told my audiences that the greatest job I ever had in my life was when I worked on a garbage route for four years to save up enough money to go to college; for it was that job that taught me this one precious lesson: It's not what I'm doing in life that gives me my self-esteem. It's the attitude I bring to what I'm doing.

I don't know where our global economy is going in the next few years. It may take the United States many years to recover. But I do believe this time of chaos and strife provides us all an opportunity to get back to the really important values in our lives. And if we do that, if we embrace those values, I believe we will become a much richer nation and world.

FINAL THOUGHTS

A Wonderful Old Fable

There is an old fable about a king who could never find contentment in his life despite the fact that he had riches beyond belief. His wizard finally told him that the only cure for him was to find a truly contented man, get his shoes, and wear them for a month. So the king sent out a party to search for just such a man. After many months, the team finally returned to announce their success.

"Did you find the contented man?" the king asked.

"Yes, O Great King, we found one," they replied.

"Then, give me his shoes so I might walk in such contentment," the king commanded.

"We can't," responded the searchers.

"And why not?" the angry king shouted.

"Because he was so poor he had no shoes to wear," came their answer.

At this point you may be standing at a crossroads. I'm sure you didn't agree with everything presented in this book, but hopefully some of it caught your attention. And just maybe some portions touched your heart. But my intent in putting this together wasn't to just bring you a little comfort. My ultimate motive is to stimulate readers to make some changes—to become lighthouses of hope for themselves and others. If you sit back now and say you will get started next week, there's about a 95 percent chance you'll end up doing nothing. You might end up like the guy in Edgar Guest's following verse.

TOMORROW

He was going to be all that a mortal should be
    Tomorrow.
No one should be kinder or braver than he
    Tomorrow.
A friend who was troubled and weary he knew,
Who'd be glad of a lift and who needed it, too;
On him he would call and see what he could do
    Tomorrow.

Each morning he stacked up the letters he'd write
    Tomorrow.
And thought of the folks he would fill with delight
    Tomorrow.
It was too bad, indeed, he was busy today,
And hadn't a minute to stop on his way;
More time he would have to give others, he'd say
    Tomorrow.

The greatest of workers this man would have been
    Tomorrow.
The world would have known him, had he ever seen
    Tomorrow.
But the fact is he died and he faded from view,
And all that he left here when living was through
Was a mountain of things he intended to do
    Tomorrow.

In my twenty-five-year career in professional speaking, my trademark has always remained the same. It's a simple thought—the final lines of a poem I wrote long ago. It reads this way: "No, life is not a bed of roses, and sometimes it's tough to see it through. But you'll never discover the best in life, until you discover the best in you." Although those words were written long ago when America was on the turnpike of prosperity, they are just as valuable today. You see, although our economy can have a strong impact on our style of life, only we, as individuals, have control of the quality of our lives. The choice is yours.

Remember

No one can teach you failure,
And no one can make you quit.
No one can force you to be negative,
Or to live like a hypocrite.

You see, the best of us all will falter,
The greatest can surely slide.
But the key to a higher living,
Is a treasure we all have inside.

It's knowing when to be flexible,
To bend but not to break.
Adapting to a world full of changes,
With our ability to give and take.

It's reflecting a sense of optimism,
Even in the shadows of despair.
It's learning to find contentment,
When you discover the cupboard is bare.

It's living with a sense of determination,
Through both the thick and the thin.
A willingness to walk the extra mile,
Where others may not have been.

No, life is not a bed of roses,
And sometimes it's tough to see it through.
But you'll never discover the best in life,
Until you discover the best in you.

by David Okerlund

For more information on The Great Depression, consider visiting the Franklin D Roosevelt Presidential Library and Museum, at 4079 Albany Post Road, Hyde Park, New York. It is one of the finest presidential libraries in the United States and has numerous gallery exhibits for your enjoyment.

CPSIA information can be obtained at www.ICGtesting.com
Printed in the USA
LVOW08s0406190615

443001LV00001B/4/P